AI JOB SHIFT

Will AI Replace *YOU?!*

Embracing Change through
EMPOWERMENT

*Transforming Fear, Uncertainty
and Doubt into*
OPPORTUNITY!

Jared A. Jacobson, Esq.

ISBN: 979-8-218-70324-0

DEDICATION

To my Three Angels, Mya - my Rock, Mom, Dad & George…
True Friends (constantly showing me how to be a better one).
My Creator.
- Jared

CONTENTS

ACKNOWLEDGMENTS

First, I would like to acknowledge and thank Stefan Youngblood – true professional, colleague and friend. I truly appreciate Stefan for welcoming me into *his* community beginning with Clubhouse in 2021, later X and LinkedIn, *putting me on* and acknowledging me as a trusted source of support and community "ally".

I'm grateful for Stefan's personal and professional mentorship, as well as providing his invaluable and sincere feedback, particularly on Chapter 9, *being honest in keeping me honest*…and sensitive to those who may not look like me or have been privileged enough to share my life experiences. Stefan is a kind, extremely intelligent, traditional, "old school", grassroots community leader, constantly innovating, learning, teaching, inspiring, supporting and bringing light to *everyone* around him, unconditionally. I strongly encourage everyone to check out Stefan's work at www.BlackAIThinktank.com www.AIStefan.com and www.HBCU.AI

I would also like to acknowledge and offer my sincere gratitude to Gary Vaynerchuck for inspiring and motivating the best parts of me, championing adaptability, evolution and extreme authenticity. Through his Veefriends universe, Gary has changed my relationship with my son and the course of *HIS* life, significantly influencing how *HE* sees the world, through positive VeeFriends' character traits, as Gary changes the world – one VeeFriends character at a time www.veefriends.com [1]

- Jared A. Jacobson

---

[1] Not to mention (while mentioning) my eternal gratitude to Gary Vee for shining a light on my son's recreation of his **favorite** VeeFriends character *Adaptable Alien!*

FORWARD

When I first picked up Jared's book, my first thrust was, *Jared was able to put his passion and knowledge on paper, or in digital 1s and 0s. Jared is a courageous, brilliant, feisty attorney who's wise enough to keep asking questions and share his brilliance with others.*

During the early days of founding the Black AI Think Tank, now the first Black AI literacy ecosystems of its kind, Jared's been in the trenches with us battling on the front lines for equity and inclusion. As a leader in the Black AI ecosystem, collaborating with everyone is high on our priority list. Not everyone steps up for that. Jared is for US. I'd highly encourage following Jared and reading, from one of the brightest and sharpest minds I know. He's a true ally. – Stefan Youngblood, Founder Black AI Thinktank, Community Leader www.BlackAIThinktank.com   www.AIStefan.com   and www.HBCU.AI.

1

INTRODUCTION

NAVIGATING THE AI REVOLUTION

*EMBRACING CHANGE WITH
CURIOSITY AND CONFIDENCE*

"Beyond this place of wrath and tears Looms but the Horror of the shade, And yet the menace of the years Finds and shall find me Unafraid" – William Ernest Henley[2]

As we stand on the precipice of the Artificial Intelligence Revolution or "AI Revolution", the air is thick with both excitement *AND* apprehension. The transformation ahead promises to reshape the very fabric of our work lives, introducing us to a world where artificial intelligence

[2] ***SEE IMAGE NOTE END OF INTRO***

partners in our daily tasks. While it's natural to fear the unknown, especially when it *appears* to threaten the security of our livelihoods, this book aims to transform that fear into a steppingstone toward **empowerment**.

By simply understanding the talents and skills you currently possess today, envisioning and learning about the roles that await tomorrow, which this book aims to help you do - you CAN bridge the gap between the present and the future, at least as far as your livelihood is concerned.

Imagine this - it's NOT just about surviving the AI Revolution…it's about *thriving* within it. Your curiosity, willingness, and desire to learn, *are* your greatest assets!

As a Lawyer practicing for more than two decades now, with a particular focus in the **Labor & Employment Law** area, I personally witness firsthand the upheavals in the job market…not to mention the profound impact that such a significant life change inevitably has on *both* the individual losing his or her job, often intertwined with their dignity, and the families struggling through the experience as a result.

I'd be remiss not to also mention the courage

demonstrated by countless clients over the years who lost their jobs for no reason other than *because* of their immutable traits (or characteristics) with which they were born, beyond their control, and regardless of their demonstrated talents and skills a/k/a work discrimination.

With the advent of AI, blue-collar, white-collar and traditionally "creative" positions are undergoing significant transformations, leaving many individuals uncertain about their future.

However, amidst the uncertainty lies **immense potential**. Despite the changing landscape, the talents and skills you possess today DO hold value. It's *not* about discarding your current skill set but rather, **simply identifying areas of interest and opportunities to evolve and thrive** in the new AI-driven world.

We are truly at the cusp of a Revolution, you are early, and **now** is the time to **seize the opportunity** to adapt and grow. Regardless of age, race, gender, education, and background, ***anyone* can leverage this moment** to transition into new company/job roles or even **start their own ventures**!

It's crucial to recognize that this Revolution impacts everyone. Contrary to initial beliefs, it's not just lower-skilled workers facing job displacement. Professionals across all sectors, **including lawyers like me**, are reevaluating their roles considering AI advancements.

In this book, we'll embark on a journey of **empowerment** and **transformation** of your mindset and expectations. We'll explore how to: assess your current skill inventory, identify emerging AI-driven opportunities, bridge the skills gap where necessary, and develop strategies to market yourself effectively and even launch your own business venture to **help others transform**!

But before we delve into the details, let's demystify some basic concepts. What is **AI, AGI, LLM**, or even a **robot**?

These terms may seem daunting. In reality, AI has already been integrated into our daily lives for years now, from smartphones to household appliances. Understanding these fundamentals is the first step towards understanding, demystifying and embracing the AI Revolution. It's actually been here, and you have been using it.

Throughout this book, the aim is to both strike a balance between **empowerment**, **inspiration**, and **motivation** on the one hand, because it IS ALL possible for You… while acknowledging the challenges ahead on the other hand.

While it's natural to feel apprehensive about the future, aiming and taking action, with at least the intention of heading in the right direction, even if not 100% on target, IS the key to progress. When you feel overwhelmed, it's *only* because you recognize the **enormous opportunities** that await you. It's a great thing and *exactly* where you want to be!

Step #1 Prioritize your opportunities

Step #2 Take Action.

If AI gives you any sense of anxiety, as David Meltzer and many others would advise, **taking action is the cure**. By the end of this journey, I hope to equip you with the confidence and resources you need to at least get started to navigate the AI Revolution successfully, providing options and opportunities for yourself, your family and your community!

So, let's embark on this journey together, embracing

the amazing opportunities that lie ahead and shaping a future where EVERYONE – regardless of what they look like, how much money they have, education level or where they were born - has a place in the AI-driven world!

***IMAGE TEXT & READING TEST*

You may notice that some of visuals/images in the book that contain text include either the **incorrect spelling, grammar…or the image is just "off" all together**!

While I *could* have continued working to fix them, it's abundantly clear **that humans are still required** to participate in this transformation "process".

By "process", I mean the **integration of AI** into our human everyday life experience. Each of us has an opportunity to participate in this process. It's helpful and necessary. All you need to do is figure out where **YOUR opportunity** is in the process. Perhaps it's related to what you do now…maybe not. That's okay either way. **CONGRATULATIONS for taking the first step** to learn more about it!

Chapter 1

AI MINDSET

*EMBRACING OPPORTUNITY - THE
COURAGE TO EVOLVE*

"The only limit to our realization of tomorrow is our doubts of today" — *Franklin D. Roosevelt*

Embracing Possibilities - The Courage to Evolve

Our mindset with which we approach the AI Revolution makes *all the difference*. Viewing this era of change as an **opportunity** rather than a threat requires **courage** and a

proactive perspective. For those worried about being left behind, remember: the first step towards the future is **believing in your ability to adapt**. Think about it – you already have or else you wouldn't be here right now! This book will guide you through shedding the fear and embracing the exciting journey of growth and learning.

Developing the right mindset involves seeing AI as a tool that **enhances**, rather than replaces our **capabilities**. Seeing AI as a tool also necessarily means tying the **development, training and supervision** of AI's not only to folks who look identical to those *doing* the development, training and supervision, but importantly, also to those who look dissimilar. It's about creating an inclusive paradigm, pushing everyone forward, not just a predetermined select group.

Embracing AI means understanding its potential to **automate mundane tasks**, allowing us to focus on creative and strategic aspects of work. It's about learning how to harness AI to innovate and solve complex problems – not replace us humans!

In embarking on this journey, it's essential to cultivate the right mindset. Regardless of your background or previous experiences, the opportunities presented by the AI Revolution are **within reach for everyone**. Allow me to share my story as an example.

At 48 years old, without any tech background or significant social media presence, I find myself facing the reality of job displacement as a lawyer. Not to mention, I received a "D" in Computer Science in college! Instead of succumbing to fear or resignation, I am personally choosing to **embrace the challenge**, recognizing the potential for **growth and adaptation** in the AI era. To be clear…it's a choice.

This transformation need not be automatic but begins with **extremely small steps**: reading this book, enrolling in free online courses, attending AI-related webinars, and connecting with professionals through social media such as LinkedIn, as well as tapping into social audio conversations on platforms like Twitter/X, or LinkedIn Audio where individuals are regularly meeting virtually to learn from each other. You can simply listen without speaking or raise your hand and ask questions. Did I mention that most of these resources are *Free 99?!* (at least for now).

I soon realized that AI isn't as intimidating as it seems. While we all have different capacities and starting points in our level of education, community, and opportunities, which is certainly not lost on me - as of the writing of this book, no one is an expert! **You are extremely early!** It's a journey of continuous learning, and every small effort builds towards significant progress.

If you are reading this right now, you too can navigate this transformative period. All it takes is the **willingness to learn** and the **determination to chart your own path**. Whether you're a seasoned professional, 18 or 65 years old, regardless of background, the AI Revolution offers opportunities for individuals of all demographics and skill sets. You simply need to find YOUR place in it.

The key is to **stay curious and open-minded**. Start by exploring free resources online as mentioned above, as well as introductory AI courses on platforms like **Coursera** and **edX**. The more you engage with the AI community, the more confident you'll become in your ability to leverage AI **however you choose**. You will also realize quickly that you don't know as little as you may think you do!

But before we dive into the practical aspects of skill assessment and career planning, let's clarify some basic definitions. **What exactly is AI**, and how does it differ from AGI (Artificial General Intelligence)? Understanding these terms is crucial for grasping the impact of AI on our lives and livelihoods. More of these terms will be discussed in the following chapters.

AI, or Artificial Intelligence, simply refers to the simulation of human intelligence by machines, enabling them to perform tasks that typically require human intelligence, such as problem-solving or decision-making. AGI, or Artificial General Intelligence on the other hand, generally represents a level of AI that exhibits human-like intelligence and versatility across various domains. Although an oversimplification, AGI can think and reason for itself. To be clear, if you were to put 10 data scientists or engineers in a room and ask them what AGI means, you would likely get 11 different answers!

More will be provided in the next chapter and throughout this book, but some examples of AI already used in daily life include virtual assistants like **Siri** and **Alexa**, which use natural language processing to understand and respond to user questions or instructions. Recommendation algorithms on platforms like **Netflix** and **Amazon** analyze your viewing and purchasing habits to suggest relevant content and products. These applications demonstrate how AI enhances user experiences by providing personalized services. **Just getting an understanding of how AI is already used can help demystify some of the fears surrounding AI**.

But AI isn't just a futuristic concept – as referenced above, AI is already deeply integrated into our daily lives. From voice assistants like Siri and Alexa to recommendation algorithms on streaming platforms, AI technologies have become ubiquitous, shaping our interactions with technology and society, whether we recognize it or not. Now you do!

As we navigate the AI Revolution, it's crucial to recognize the opportunities and challenges it presents. While the prospect of job displacement may be daunting, it's also an **opportunity for personal and professional growth**. By adopting a **growth mindset** and embracing lifelong learning, you absolutely CAN position yourself for success in the AI-driven world. Don't forget, you are

adaptable, that's why you are here.

AI's integration into various sectors means that **any and all skills related to AI are in high demand**. For example, **simply understanding** how AI can improve healthcare through predictive analytics or enhance marketing strategies through data-driven insights can set you apart in your field. The ability to stay positive, adapt and the willingness to learn continuously is the **most valuable skill** in the AI era.

So, let's approach this journey with **optimism** and **determination**, knowing that the future holds **unlimited possibilities** and **opportunities** for those willing to adapt and evolve. Together, we'll explore how to assess your current skills, identify emerging opportunities, and chart a course towards a thriving future in the AI era.

Remember, *every significant journey starts with a single step*. Whether it's learning a new AI tool, attending a workshop, or reading a book on AI (as you are literally doing now), each step will bring you closer to mastering the skills needed for the future. Embrace the change with **confidence, enthusiasm and curiosity**, and you'll discover a **world of opportunities waiting for you**.

"Your mindset determines your future" — *Anonymous*

Chapter 2

DEMYSTEFYING AI

IT'S NOT THAT DEEP

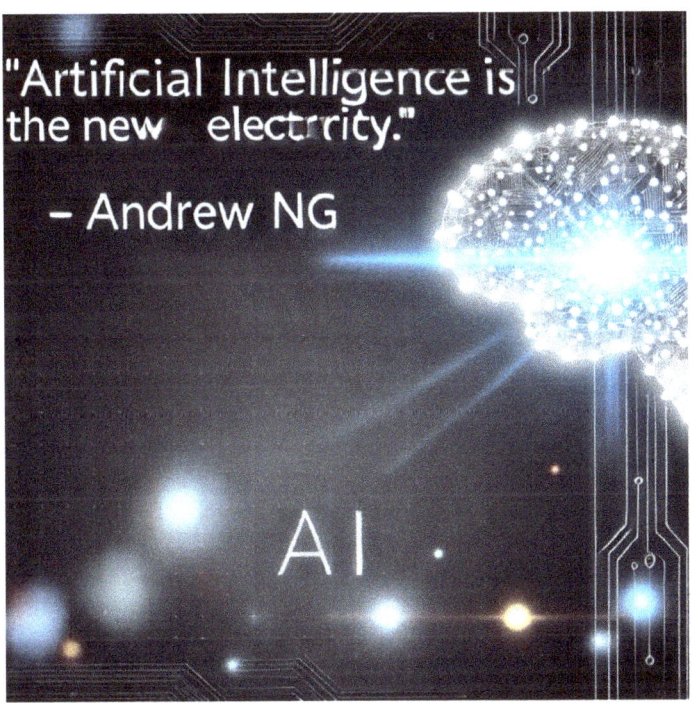

"The science of today is the technology of tomorrow" —
& Edward Telle

Additional Helpful – Basic "AI" Definitions

To lower the barrier to entry and foster a deeper understanding of AI, it's essential to clarify some fundamental terms in a simple, relatable manner:

AI (Artificial Intelligence): The simulation of human

intelligence in machines programmed to think and learn. AI encompasses various subfields such as machine learning, neural networks, and natural language processing. AI systems can perform tasks like visual perception, speech recognition, decision-making, and language translation.

AGI (Artificial General Intelligence): A hypothetical AI that possesses the ability to understand, learn, and apply its intelligence across a wide range of tasks, akin to human cognitive abilities. AGI, depending on who you ask, possibly still remains a theoretical concept, as current AI systems are specialized and lack the general cognitive abilities of humans…as far as we are aware. The development of AGI would signify a major breakthrough, enabling machines to perform any intellectual task that a human can. Regardless of various opinions, the general consensus is that we are certainly not 100% "there" as of the publication date of this book.

LLM (Large Language Models): AI systems are designed to understand and generate human-like text based on vast amounts of data. LLMs (think OpenAI / ChatGPT and Google's Gemini) are trained on diverse datasets, enabling them to generate coherent and contextually relevant text…most of the time. They are used in applications such as chatbots, automated content creation, and language translation services. You may have encountered some version of an LLM when interacting with a "customer service agent" when calling a large company. These days, you can generally still tell. In the future, it will be extremely difficult to distinguish between an AI bot and a human being. AI Influencers on social media are rapidly becoming a "thing".

Robot: A machine programmed to perform tasks autonomously, often used in manufacturing, household chores, or exploration. Robots can range from simple mechanical devices to sophisticated machines with AI capabilities. They are employed in various industries, including automotive manufacturing, healthcare (surgical robots), and space exploration (rovers and drones).

Machine Learning (ML): A subset of AI that involves training algorithms to recognize patterns in data and make predictions or decisions without explicit programming. Examples include spam filters and recommendation systems.

Deep Learning: A subset of machine learning that uses neural networks with many layers (deep neural networks) to analyze complex data patterns. It is used in image and speech recognition.

Neural Network: A computational model inspired by the human brain's network of neurons. It consists of interconnected nodes (neurons) that process and transmit information, used in various AI applications.

Natural Language Processing (NLP): A field of AI that focuses on the interaction between computers and humans using natural language. It enables machines to understand, interpret, and generate human language. Examples include virtual assistants and language translation services.

Algorithm: A set of rules or instructions given to an AI system to help it learn and make decisions. Algorithms are the building blocks of AI, determining how data is processed. As you are likely aware, the algorithms or "algos" are already exerting significant influence over society in the social media space – reliably feeding you more of what you have previously expressed interest in seeing.

Data Mining: The process of discovering patterns and knowledge from large amounts of data. It involves methods at the intersection of machine learning, statistics, and database systems.

Autonomous Vehicles: Vehicles equipped with AI systems capable of sensing their environment and operating without human intervention. Examples include self-driving cars and drones. As you are likely aware, Tesla is at the forefront of self-driving autonomous vehicles. Regardless of whether or not you would personally ride in one or your opinion as to whether the public roads are "ready" for autonomous vehicles, what's clear is that they have arrived.

Computer Vision: A field of AI that enables computers to interpret and make decisions based on visual input from the world. It is used in facial recognition, object detection, and medical imaging. If you use "face ID" on any of your devices, you understand.

Chatbot: An AI program designed to simulate conversation with human users, especially over the internet. Chatbots are used in customer service, virtual assistants, and online help systems. Yes, they can be *extremely* frustrating, but they are improving rapidly.

Through these definitions and everyday examples (*e.g.*, smartphones, microwaves, vacuum cleaners), I **aim to make AI approachable**, illustrating its long-standing presence in our lives.

It's normal and suggested that you **go back and re-read** the above definitions as much as necessary. Understanding these terms helps demystify AI and highlights its pervasive role in our daily lives. From the recommendation algorithms on Netflix to the facial recognition software on smartphones, AI technologies are already integral to modern living. By grasping these basics, you can better appreciate the transformative potential of AI and its applications in various fields.

"AI is not about replacing humans, it's about augmenting human capabilities" — Satya Nadella

Chapter 3

DISAPPEARING JOBS & EMERGING OPPORTUNITIES

YOUR OPPORTUNITY IS RIGHT IN FRONT OF YOU!

TRANSITION IS NOT A THREAT
BUT AN OPPORRTUNITY TO RENNVEN YOURSELF

"In the middle of difficulty lies opportunity" — *Albert Einstein*

Navigating the Shift

As we confront the realities of the AI Revolution, it's essential to understand how the job market is evolving. Traditional roles are undergoing transformations, while **new opportunities are emerging** in their wake.

It's undeniable that the AI Revolution has, is and will

continue to transform industries at an unprecedented pace. While some jobs are becoming obsolete, **new and innovative roles are being created**. It's crucial to stay informed about these changes and be proactive in adapting to the new landscape. Start small - perhaps visit one resource daily for five minutes, to learn these developments!

It's true - jobs that were once considered stable and secure are now at risk of displacement. From doctors and lawyers to writers and administrative professionals - no sector is immune to the impact of AI-driven automation. Blue-collar workers, including factory workers (think Amazon) and truck drivers, are also facing significant changes as automation technologies continue to advance.

For example, AI-powered diagnostic tools are **assisting** doctors, reducing the need for certain routine tasks. Similarly, legal software can now handle document review, affecting paralegal and junior lawyer positions. In manufacturing, robots are taking over repetitive tasks, while autonomous vehicles are transforming the logistics and transportation sectors.

However, amidst the uncertainty of disappearing jobs

lies a **realm of possibilities**. The **AI Revolution is not just about job displacement**; it's also about job **creation**. New roles and industries are emerging, driven by advancements in AI, machine learning, and automation. **You could literally create your own role** once you understand the direction in which we are heading! As Wayne Gretzky has famously said "***skate to where the hockey puck is heading, not where it is***".

New job categories such as **AI trainers, data annotators, and ethical AI officers** are becoming essential. These roles require a mix of technical knowledge and soft skills, highlighting the importance of **adaptability and continuous learning**. For instance, data scientists and machine learning engineers are in high demand to develop and maintain AI systems.

In the AI-driven world, roles such as **data scientists, AI ethicists, and automation specialists** are in high demand. These positions require a combination of technical expertise, critical thinking skills, and adaptability—the very qualities that **individuals can cultivate** to thrive in the AI era.

Other emerging roles include **AI product managers**,

who oversee the development and implementation of AI solutions, and **AI policy advisors**, who help create regulations and guidelines for AI usage. The rise of AI also fosters **entrepreneurship**, offering **opportunities to innovate and create new business** models around AI technologies. It's these **supportive roles** that often rise to the forefront.

But **how do you navigate this shift** from disappearing jobs to **emerging opportunities?** It starts with a thorough **assessment of your current skills** and a **comparison with the skills required** for new AI-driven roles of which we are currently aware AND those skills and roles of which no one has even dreamt…perhaps it will be **You!**

Begin by listing your interests, talents, current skills and experiences. Identify areas where you can transfer your existing skills to new roles. For instance, a background in **statistics** can be valuable in data science, while **project management** experience can be useful for AI project management roles. Look for online courses, certifications, and workshops to bridge any skill gaps. Many are free.

By comparing the skills required for current jobs with

those needed for emerging AI-driven roles, individuals can **identify areas of alignment and potential opportunities** for growth and transition. This exercise underscores the importance of continuous learning and adaptation in the face of technological advancements.

Embrace lifelong learning by enrolling in AI and machine learning courses on the platforms previously mentioned. YouTube is also a great source of information and education. When unsure, **ask for help**... and then **ask again**! I've found that people ahead of us always want to help.

"The future belongs to those who prepare for it today"
— Malcolm X

Chapter 4

HUMANS & AI – SYMBIOTIC RELATIONSHIP

IT'S NOT AN "EITHER/OR" BUT AN "AND"…

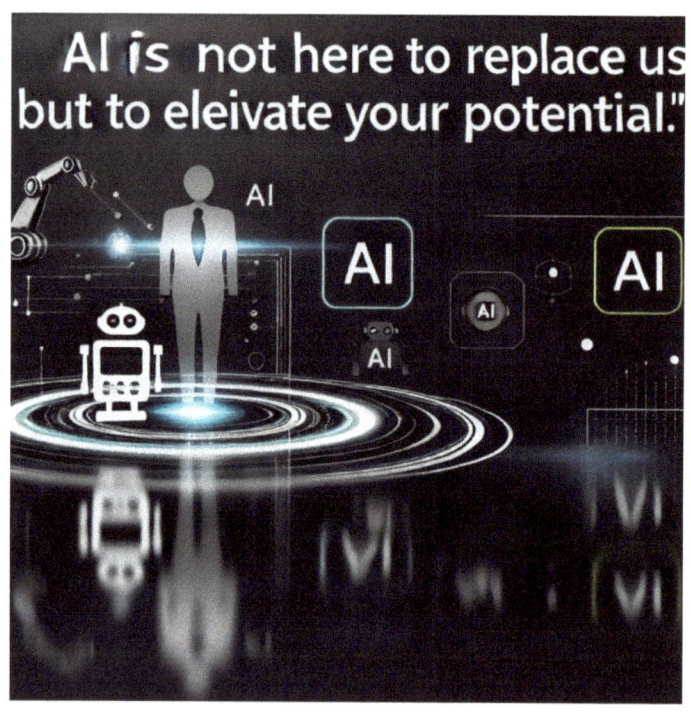

"Fortune Favors the Bold" - Anonymous

Working Together to Benefit Each Other

As the integration of AI into various industries continues to accelerate, it's not unexpected that many individuals from all walks of life will express concern about AI taking over jobs and rendering human roles obsolete. However, this chapter aims to dispel these fears by illustrating the

indispensable role humans play in the development and functioning of AI.

By embracing an open mindset and viewing AI as a **complementary, supplemental and supportive tool** rather than a threat, we can foster a mutually beneficial relationship that enhances both human capabilities and AI performance. Put simply – **it's a collaborative effort**. AI can help us in SO many ways. We just need to learn how to help AI help each one of us!

The Importance of an Open Mindset

Adaptability and Growth: Embracing change and technology fosters personal and professional growth. Those who remain adaptable and open to learning new skills will find themselves better equipped to collaborate with AI. Keep in mind – IF you are reading this right now, **you are WAY ahead of the game!**

Innovation and Creativity: Human creativity and intuition are irreplaceable. AI can process vast amounts of data and provide insights using predictions, but **it is the human mind that can think outside the box and innovate**.

Mutual Learning: Humans Teaching AI

Training AI Systems: Humans are essential in training AI models by providing data, correcting errors, and refining algorithms. This continuous interaction ensures that AI systems improve over time.

Ethical Considerations: Human oversight is crucial in ensuring that AI systems operate ethically and do not reinforce biases. This involves monitoring AI behavior and making necessary adjustments. Simply by **"playing around"** and using AI, paying attention and noticing what responses we get based on our inquiries, or "prompts" as they are called, depending on the LLM model, we are often **teaching it how to respond**.

Depending on your demographic, and level of interest of course, discussed further throughout this book, YOUR role in helping AI learn could be much more valuable than you may have previously imagined! Just YOUR involvement could affect tons of generations that follow.

Imagine this – you ask an AI like ChatGPT to create an image of a corporate executive for a book or project on which you are working…and it comes back with a white male 10/10 times. You *could* hit the "thumbs down" button to the response, notifying OpenAI of your concern…or perhaps give it a "thumbs up" if you are a White Nationalist…depending on who is reading this. Either way, **your contribution does make a difference**.

AI Enhancing Human Capabilities

Augmenting Productivity: AI can handle repetitive and time-consuming tasks, allowing humans to focus on more complex and strategic activities, including supervising the AI to confirm that it is in fact performing it's assigned tasks…which is a separate job from programming it to perform the tasks! Combining both of these new high-demand jobs leads to increased productivity and job **satisfaction**.

Data-Driven Decision Making: AI provides valuable insights from large datasets on which it has been trained, that would be impossible for humans to process manually. This enhances decision-making processes in various fields, from healthcare to finance, which can be utilized by CEOs and AI beginners alike with just a simple prompt used to get a response from an AI. [3]The great news is that if the AI does not give you a helpful answer, nothing stops you from trying again, learning how to prompt the AI with greater accuracy and getting a more accurate response.

Those who have become somewhat proficient in this practice of *playing around* may be referred to as "**Prompt Engineers**". It's a small leap from learning how to better prompt an AI to get better responses for yourself, to applying for a job at a growing company or starting your own Prompt Engineering company to help other companies grow! To be clear, Prompt Engineers are currently earning greater than $100,000/year annually.

Addressing Apprehensions

Job Transformation, Not Elimination: While AI may automate certain tasks, it also creates new job opportunities. Roles that require **emotional intelligence,**

---

[3] How valuable might these "valuable insights" be for the companies themselves that choose to deploy them? What might be the potential impact on society? Whether you are thinking *positive* or *negative*, and I'll reserve my opinion for the time being…BONUS points for starting a blog or new YouTube channel discussing your perspective. First mover opportunity here.

critical thinking, and **interpersonal skills** remain in demand.

Continuous Learning: The dynamic nature of AI means that continuous learning and upskilling are vital. Although not the subject of this book, education systems and workplaces need to adapt by offering training programs that align with technological advancements.

The Future of Human-AI Collaboration

Symbiotic Synergy: The relationship between humans and AI can be described as symbiotic and synergistic. Each party enhances the other's capabilities, leading to a more efficient and innovative ecosystem.

AI as a Partner: Viewing AI as a partner rather than a competitor encourages collaboration. This mindset shift is crucial for maximizing the benefits of AI integration.

The future of work is not about humans versus AI but **humans working alongside AI**. By fostering a symbiotic relationship, we can harness the strengths of both humans and AI to create a more productive, innovative, and inclusive world. Embracing this partnership with an open mindset will pave the way for a future where technology and humanity thrive together.

We question all of our beliefs, <u>except</u> for the ones that we <u>really</u> believe in...and those we never think to question" – Orson Scott Card, often quoted by Alex Hormozi

Chapter 5

SKILLS ASSESSMENT

*WHERE WE ARE HAS NOTHING TO DO
WITH WHERE WE CHOOSE TO GO*

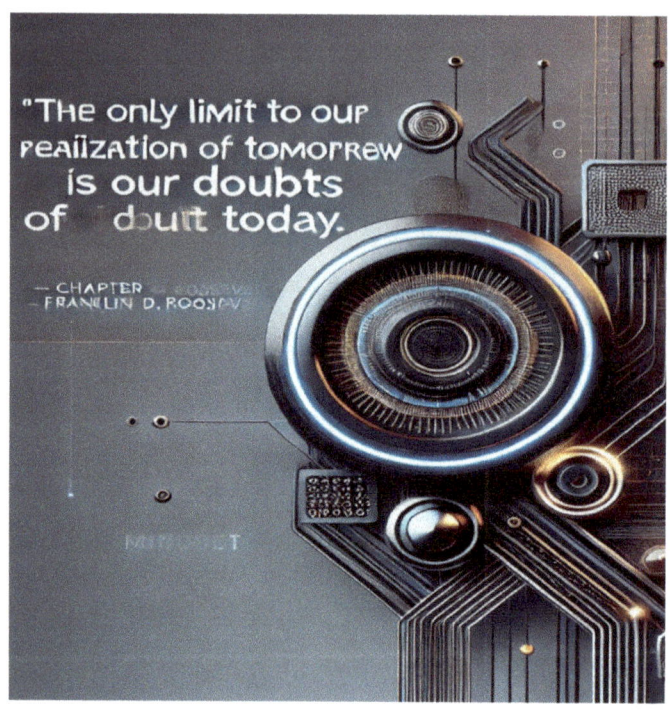

"The only limit to our realization of tomorrow is our doubts of doubt today."

— CHAPTER
— FRANKLIN D. ROOSEVELT

"The best investment you can make is in yourself" —
Warren Buffett

Taking Inventory of Your Current Skills

Before you can chart a course towards new opportunities, it's essential to take stock of your current skill set. What are your strengths, weaknesses, and areas for improvement? Consider both **hard/technical skills**, such as programming languages or data analysis AND **soft skills**, such as communication, problem-solving / conflict resolution, emotional intelligence or "EQ". They are **equally valuable in the AI Revolution!**

Interestingly, while the perfect mix of prediction and modeling may appear to many (certainly less day by day) as superior emotional intelligence — understanding, empathy and compassion....I'm not aware of any AI or robot that currently possesses or is expected to actually possess these "soft skills" anytime soon.

Conducting a thorough skills assessment can **reveal hidden strengths** and potential areas for growth. Use self-assessment tools and seek feedback from colleagues or mentors to gain a comprehensive view of your capabilities. Document your skills in categories such as **technical, analytical, creative,** and **interpersonal**.

Take a moment to reflect on your professional **experiences** and **achievements**. Putting aside whether you enjoyed them, with the intention of remaining objective for the purpose of this reflective thought exercise - what tasks or projects have you actually **excelled** at in the past? Go back as far as you need to.

What skills have you developed through your education, work and experiences? Then consider your talents, interests and hobbies.

Create a simple portfolio that showcases your work and achievements. Include detailed descriptions of your roles, responsibilities, and the outcomes of your projects. Highlight any instances where you utilized innovative solutions or demonstrated leadership. **These skills are at a premium in the AI Revolution**.

Creating an inventory of your skills will provide a foundation for identifying potential areas of **alignment with emerging AI-driven roles**.

Use online platforms like LinkedIn to compare your skills with those in demand in your industry. This will help you understand where you stand and what additional **skills** you may need to acquire. Update your inventory monthly or quarterly to reflect new skills and experiences.

"Know your strengths and limitations and leverage them to your advantage" — Anonymous

Chapter 6

IDENTIFY *YOUR* AI OPPORTUNITY

YOUR OPPORTUNITY IN THE AI REVOLUTION

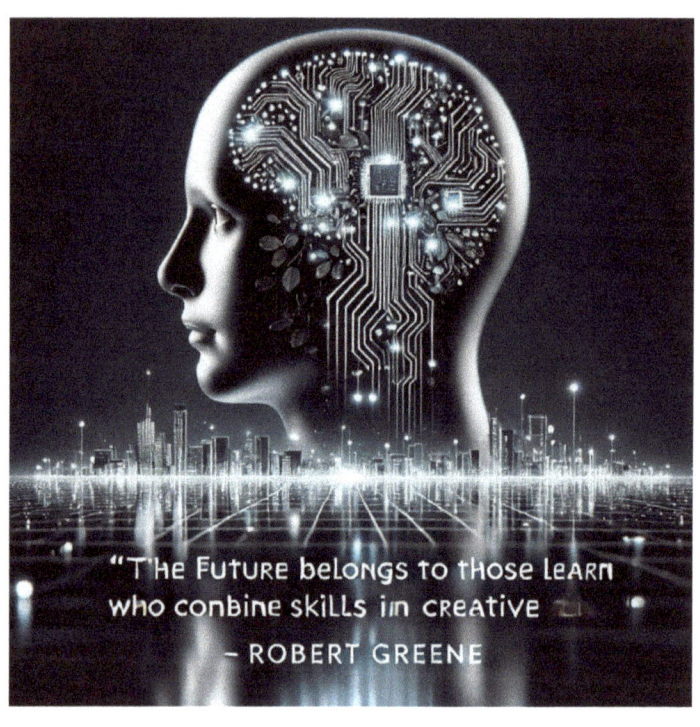

"THe FuTuRe beLoNgs To THose LeaRn who conbine skiLLs in cReaTive – ROBERT GREENE

"Opportunities don't happen, you create them" —
Chris Grosser

Comparing Skillset with New AI Jobs

Once you've assessed your current skills, it's time to explore the landscape of emerging AI-driven opportunities. Research job trends and industry forecasts to gain insight into the skills and qualifications sought after in the AI era. When searching, use keywords contained within descriptions of your own past experiences, skills, interests and hobbies.

Leverage **resources** like job boards, industry reports, and professional networks to stay informed about the latest trends in AI. Attend webinars and conferences to gain firsthand insights from industry experts. Remember, free AI training courses are available.

Look for roles that align with your strengths and interests while also considering areas where you may need to develop new skills or knowledge. Keep in mind that the AI Revolution is not limited to technical roles — **opportunities exist across diverse sectors and disciplines**.

Consider roles that would naturally incorporate and bridge your current expertise and interests with emerging AI technologies. For example, if you have a background in marketing, explore roles in AI-driven digital marketing or customer analytics. If you're in healthcare, look into AI applications in medical diagnostics or health informatics. Moving forward, AI will be both intertwined within every industry as well as present in industry-supporting roles. Allow yourself to

"think outside the box".

Consider the following questions as you explore potential opportunities:

◊ What are the key skills and qualifications required for AI-driven roles **in my/desired field**?

◊ How do **my current skills, experiences and interests** align with these requirements?

◊ Are there areas where I need to acquire **new skills or knowledge** to remain competitive in the job market?

Create a simple personal development plan outlining the steps you need to take to acquire the necessary skills you desire to acquire the job you may be seeking or the services you may wish to offer. This may include enrolling in online courses, obtaining certifications, or gaining practical experience through projects and internships.

By **comparing your current skills, experiences and interests with the requirements of emerging AI-driven roles**, you can identify areas of alignment and potential areas for growth.

Embrace continuous learning by setting aside time

each week to study new AI technologies and their applications. Start as small as one (1) hour per week or **20 minutes per day**. Join online communities and forums mentioned throughout this book to discuss trends, share knowledge, seek advice from peers and professionals in the field…or just listen and learn.

"Seize the opportunities that life offers you" — *Anonymous*

Chapter 7

BRIDGING THE AI GAP –
A PRACTICAL GUIDE

IT'S EASIER THAN YOU THINK....

"The journey of a thousand miles begins with one step"
— Lao Tzu

From Old Jobs to New AI Opportunities

Example 1: *From Retail Salesperson to Virtual Shopping Consultant*

◊ **Current Job Skills:** Customer service, product knowledge, sales techniques.

◊ **AI Revolution Role:** Virtual Shopping Consultants will use AI tools to provide personalized shopping experiences online, leveraging chatbots, virtual reality, and data analytics to cater to customer preferences.

◊ **Bridging the Gap:** The fundamental skills of understanding customer needs and product expertise remain vital, enriched by learning to manage AI-powered platforms.

Virtual Shopping Consultants will also need to understand AI-driven recommendation systems and virtual reality interfaces. Training in these areas can enhance their ability to provide a seamless and personalized shopping experience. **Can you think of ways to improve someone's shopping experience?**

Example 2*: From Taxi Driver to Autonomous Vehicle Fleet Coordinator*

◊ **Current Job Skills:** Navigation, vehicle maintenance knowledge, customer service.

◊ **AI Revolution Role:** Coordinators will oversee fleets of autonomous vehicles, managing logistics, scheduling, and remote troubleshooting.

◊ **Bridging the Gap:** The transition focuses on leveraging logistical and customer service skills, with additional training in technology management and remote operations.

Fleet Coordinators will also need to be proficient in using AI-powered fleet management software and understanding the regulatory framework for autonomous vehicles. Certification programs in autonomous vehicle management can provide the necessary skills. **Could you create and sell / license your own software adding one small feature to this process?**

Example 3: *From Human Resources Manager to AI Integration Specialist*

◊ **Current Job Skills:** People management, recruitment, policy development.

◊ **AI Revolution Role:** Specialists will guide the integration of AI tools in the workplace, focusing on training programs, ethical AI use, and enhancing team productivity through technology.

◊ **Bridging the Gap:** Building on strong interpersonal skills and organizational policies knowledge, with added focus on AI technology's implications and applications in the workplace.

AI Integration Specialists will need to stay updated on the latest AI tools and their applications in HR. Workshops and certifications in AI ethics and technology integration can provide the necessary knowledge. **Do you currently have any experience with HR matters?**

Example 4*: From Administrative Assistant to AI Administrative Coordinator*

◊ **Current Job Skills:** Organizational skills, communication, time management, proficiency in office software (*e.g.,* Microsoft Office Suite, Google Workspace).

◊ **AI Revolution Role:** AI Administrative Coordinators will use AI tools to automate scheduling, manage communications, and optimize workflow efficiency.

◊ **Bridging the Gap:** Leverage existing organizational and communication skills while learning to operate and integrate AI-based office management tools.

AI Administrative Coordinators should also familiarize themselves with AI-powered project management tools and virtual assistants. Training in these areas can enhance their efficiency and effectiveness in managing office operations. **Do you have any experience using Microsoft Word and Google Docs?**

Example 5: From Factory Worker to AI Maintenance Technician

◊ **Current Job Skills:** Manual dexterity, attention to detail, ability to operate machinery, knowledge of safety protocols.

◊ **AI Revolution Role:** AI Maintenance Technicians will oversee the maintenance and repair of automated machinery, using AI for diagnostics and predictive maintenance.

◊ **Bridging the Gap:** Build on machinery operation skills by learning AI diagnostic tools and predictive maintenance technologies.

AI Maintenance Technicians should also gain skills in troubleshooting AI systems and understanding the integration of AI with industrial machinery. Certifications in industrial AI maintenance can provide the necessary expertise. **Do you currently possess a "technician" mindset that may be applied to the AI space?**

Example 6: *From Truck Driver to Autonomous Fleet Manager*

◊ **Current Job Skills:** Driving proficiency, navigation, logistics management, ability to adhere to regulations and safety standards.

◊ **AI Revolution Role:** Autonomous Fleet Managers will supervise fleets of self-driving trucks, handling logistics, routing, and compliance.

◊ **Bridging the Gap:** Transition logistics management skills to oversee autonomous systems, gaining knowledge in AI navigation and fleet management software.

Autonomous Fleet Managers will also need to understand AI-driven logistics optimization and remote monitoring systems. Training in these areas can enhance their ability to manage autonomous fleets effectively. **Truckdrivers - who may understand better than you how to improve autonomous fleets based on your own personal experience?**

Example 7: From Customer Service Representative to AI Customer Experience Specialist

◊ **Current Job Skills:** Communication skills, problem-solving, empathy, ability to handle customer inquiries and complaints effectively.

◊ **AI Revolution Role:** AI Customer Experience Specialists will utilize AI-driven chatbots and analytics to enhance customer service and personalize interactions.

◊ **Bridging the Gap:** Enhance customer service skills with training in AI tools and customer data analytics to provide tailored support.

AI Customer Experience Specialists should also understand the integration of AI with Customer/Client Relationship Management or "CRM" systems and data-driven customer insights. Certifications in AI customer experience management can provide the necessary skills. **Have you ever interacted with customers on behalf of your own or someone else's business?**

Example 8: From Teacher to AI Educational Technologist

◊ **Current Job Skills:** Subject matter expertise, classroom management, lesson planning,

◊ communication, patience.

◊ **AI Revolution Role:** AI Educational Technologists will develop and implement AI-based learning tools, personalized education plans, and virtual classrooms.

◊ **Bridging the Gap:** Utilize teaching experience to create AI-driven educational content and platforms, focusing on adaptive learning technologies.

AI Educational Technologists should also stay updated on the latest AI educational tools and their applications in personalized learning. Workshops and certifications in AI educational technology can provide the necessary knowledge. **Have you ever learned something new and taught those just starting out?**

***Example 9**: From Retail Sales Associate to AI Retail Analyst*

◊ **Current Job Skills:** Customer service, product knowledge, sales techniques, cash handling.

◊ **AI Revolution Role:** AI Retail Analysts will use data analytics and AI tools to optimize inventory, predict trends, and enhance customer engagement.

◊   **Bridging the Gap:** Transition sales techniques to analyze customer data and trends, mastering AI tools for inventory and sales optimization.

AI Retail Analysts should also understand the integration of AI with retail management systems and predictive analytics. Training in these areas can enhance their ability to optimize retail operations effectively. **Have you ever managed a retail store?**

Example 10: *From Healthcare Nurse to AI Health Data Analyst*

◊   **Current Job Skills:** Clinical skills (*e.g.,* administering medication, wound care), empathy, critical thinking, attention to detail.

◊   **AI Revolution Role:** AI Health Data Analysts will analyze patient data to improve care, using AI for predictive diagnostics and personalized treatment plans.

◊   **Bridging the Gap:** Leverage clinical expertise while gaining skills in data analytics and AI-driven health informatics.

AI Health Data Analysts should also understand the integration of AI with electronic health records and predictive diagnostics. Certifications in AI health data analytics can provide. **Nurses – are you able to display empathy and compassion while keeping track of a patient's health condition?**

Example 11: From Construction Worker to AI Construction Coordinator

◊ **Current Job Skills:** Physical strength, knowledge of construction materials and methods, ability to read blueprints, teamwork.

◊ **AI Revolution Role:** AI Construction Coordinators will oversee construction projects using AI for project planning, resource allocation, and safety monitoring.

◊ **Bridging the Gap:** Build on construction knowledge by learning AI-based project management and safety monitoring tools.

AI Construction Coordinators should also familiarize themselves with AI-powered design software and construction drones. Training in these areas can enhance their ability to plan and monitor projects efficiently. **If you understand how to put a project together, could you learn a new AI-powered software program to help**

make your job easier?

Example 12: *From Retail Manager to AI Inventory Management Specialist*

◊ **Current Job Skills:** Inventory control, team leadership, customer service, sales strategies.

◊ **AI Revolution Role:** AI Inventory Management Specialists will utilize AI to monitor stock levels, forecast demand, and optimize supply chain logistics.

◊ **Bridging the Gap:** Transition management and inventory control skills by learning AI tools for predictive analytics and automated supply chain management.

AI Inventory Management Specialists should also understand the integration of AI with Enterprise Retail Planning or "ERP" systems and real-time data analytics. Certifications in supply chain management and AI logistics can provide the necessary skills. **Do you have experience managing inventory?**

Example 13: *From Financial Analyst to AI Financial Planner*

◊ **Current Job Skills:** Financial analysis, budgeting,

forecasting, financial reporting.

◊ **AI Revolution Role:** AI Financial Planners will use AI-driven tools to create personalized financial plans, automate investment strategies, and provide real-time financial advice.

◊ **Bridging the Gap:** Enhance financial analysis skills with AI-driven financial planning software and automated investment management tools.

AI Financial Planners should also familiarize themselves with AI-powered investment platforms and "robo-advisors". Training in these areas can enhance their ability to provide tailored financial advice and investment strategies. **Do you have the ability to learn and deploy superior data-supported "opinions" in order to achieve superior client results?**

Example 14*: From Librarian to AI Data Curator*

◊ **Current Job Skills:** Information management, research, cataloging, organization.

◊ **AI Revolution Role:** AI Data Curators will organize and manage large datasets, ensuring data quality and accessibility for AI training.

◊ **Bridging the Gap:** Leverage existing information

management skills while learning data annotation and AI training techniques.

AI Data Curators should also understand the integration of AI with data management systems and metadata tagging. Certifications in data management and AI data curation can provide the necessary skills. **Do you have experience organizing information in any industry or in your personal life?**

Example 15*: From Graphic Designer to AI User Experience (UX) Designer*

◊ **Current Job Skills:** Visual design, creativity, software proficiency (*e.g.*, Adobe Creative Suite), user interface design.

◊ **AI Revolution Role:** AI UX Designers will create user-friendly interfaces for AI applications, ensuring seamless user experiences.

◊ **Bridging the Gap:** Enhance design skills by understanding AI capabilities and user behavior analytics to improve interface design.

AI UX Designers should also familiarize themselves with AI-powered design tools and usability testing software. Training in these areas can enhance their ability to create intuitive and effective user interfaces. **Are you creative and interested in participating in the creation of AI and shaping how it interacts with humans for an unknown timeframe?**

Example 16: From Accountant to AI Financial Analyst

◊ **Current Job Skills:** Financial reporting, budgeting, auditing, tax preparation.

◊ **AI Revolution Role:** AI Financial Analysts will utilize AI tools for real-time financial analysis, predictive analytics, and automated reporting.

◊ **Bridging the Gap:** Transition accounting skills to incorporate AI-driven financial tools and data analytics for enhanced financial decision-making.

AI Financial Analysts should also understand the integration of AI with financial management systems and predictive analytics. Certifications in AI financial analysis can provide the necessary skills. **Could you learn how to utilize AI to improve upon what you currently do in significantly *less* time and with significantly *more* accuracy?**

Example 17: From Marketing Manager to AI Marketing Strategist

◊ **Current Job Skills:** Campaign management, market analysis, branding, digital marketing.

◊ **AI Revolution Role:** AI Marketing Strategists will develop and execute marketing strategies using AI for customer segmentation, trend analysis, and personalized marketing.

◊ **Bridging the Gap:** Build on marketing expertise by mastering AI tools for data-driven marketing and customer insights.

AI Marketing Strategists should also familiarize themselves with AI-powered marketing platforms and customer analytics tools. Training in these areas can enhance their ability to develop and implement effective marketing strategies. **If you already know how to create organic (personal or professional) social media marketing videos, campaigns...could you devote a limited number of hours to learn how to utilize a tool that does it all for you in significantly less time, while you focus your energy elsewhere?**

Example 18: From Legal Assistant to AI Legal Technologist

◊ **Current Job Skills:** Legal research, document preparation, client communication, case management.

◊ **AI Revolution Role:** AI Legal Technologists will develop and manage AI applications for legal research, document automation, and case analysis.

◊ **Bridging the Gap:** Leverage legal knowledge while learning to integrate AI tools to streamline legal processes and improve efficiency.

AI Legal Technologists should also understand the integration of AI with legal research databases and document management systems. Certifications in legal technology and AI applications can provide the necessary skills. **Could you start a business helping lawyers utilize this technology?**

Example 19: From Journalist to AI Content Strategist

◊ **Current Job Skills:** Writing, editing, research, interviewing, storytelling.

◊ **AI Revolution Role:** AI Content Strategists will use AI to analyze content performance, generate insights, and optimize content strategies across platforms.

◊ **Bridging the Gap:** Enhance storytelling and editorial skills with AI-driven content analytics and strategy optimization tools.

AI Content Strategists should also familiarize themselves with AI-powered content creation tools and performance analytics platforms. Training in these areas can enhance their ability to develop and execute effective content strategies. **Could you utilize AI to both improve your own creativity and offer services to others helping them to do the same?**

Example 20*: From Event Planner to AI Event Experience Designer*

◊ **Current Job Skills:** Event coordination, project management, vendor negotiation, customer service.

◊ **AI Revolution Role:** AI Event Experience Designers will utilize AI to personalize event experiences, manage logistics, and enhance attendee engagement through data insights.

◊ **Bridging the Gap:** Build on event planning expertise by adopting AI tools for personalized event management and real-time data analysis.

AI Event Experience Designers should also understand the integration of AI with event management software and attendee engagement platforms. Certifications in AI event management can provide the necessary skills. Could you learn to utilize AI to automate repetitive daily tasks while you spend your high value time offering services to potential customers as an owner or employee?

"Bridging the gap between where you are and where you want to be starts with a single step" — Anonymous

Chapter 8

ENTREPRENEURIAL JOURNEY

YOU ARE EARLY - NO-BODY IS AN EXPERT....

The future is not to to be feared but be shaped our vision and actions.

"The way to get started is to quit talking and begin doing" — Walt Disney

Empowerment to Start Your OWN Company

While this book is focused *primarily* on job transition into the AI Revolution, if you haven't realized, the information contained in this book is ***equally* applicable to anyone looking to start their own business**, perform services or offer a product, requiring the **same process** to identify the skills necessary to deliver those valuable services or product, to any individual or business.

In fact, now that **_YOU_** do **_HAVE_** the knowledge (and clearly the **_ABILITY_**) to at least learn any of these new skills, learning how to become an entrepreneur and run a successful business might be the next natural step for you!

Starting a business requires additional skills but is **_EASILY_** within reach for individuals LIKE **_YOU_** READING THIS NOW—willing to **learn and adapt** which are the **primary** skills you are literally learning to develop NOW! That's the point.

Put simply – deliver a product or service, let people know you are able to do that through effective marketing, and use a simple payment processing system to accept payment, _e.g._, PayPal, Venmo, Zelle, or any other payment processor. Period.

Some key skills for entrepreneurship include:

1. Business Acumen:

◊ **_Understanding Market Trends:_** Stay informed about the latest industry trends, market demands, and technological advancements (AI can help you automate this by delivering daily updates from your favorite sources...**what sources do the leaders in the industry follow?**). This knowledge will help you make informed business decisions. **Ask AI.**

◊ ***Customer Needs:*** Conduct surveys, focus groups, and market research to understand your target audience's needs and preferences. Ask your clients and throw out questions on social media to get feedback on any new ideas – disregard any criticism and implement any positive suggestions. This will enable you to tailor your products and services to meet those needs (think AI), guided by real-time market needs. **Ask AI.**

◊ ***Competitive Landscapes:*** Analyze your competitors to identify their strengths and weaknesses. Use this information to differentiate your business and gain a competitive edge. **What can you do differently** to better assist YOUR clients? (think AI). **Ask AI.**

2. Financial Literacy:

◊ ***Budgeting:*** Create a detailed budget that outlines

your expected income and expenses. How much can you charge each client and how much will it cost you to deliver the product or service (all-in, to the extent predictable). This will help you manage your finances effectively and avoid overspending. **Ask AI.**

◊ *Financial Forecasting:* Use financial forecasting tools to predict future revenue and expenses. This will help you plan for growth and make strategic investments. **Ask AI.**

◊ *Managing Cash Flow:* Monitor your cash flow regularly to ensure you have enough funds to cover your expenses to continue acquiring customers and delivering a superior service or product. Implement strategies to improve cash flow, such as offering discounts for early payments or negotiating better payment terms with suppliers. Ask AI.

By identifying and/or equipping yourself with the skills and mindset needed for entrepreneurship, you can explore the possibility of **starting your own ventures** and contributing to the evolving landscape of the AI-driven world.

Once you learn how to work with AI, no longer intimidated by the thought of it, those technical skills can be **extremely useful in running your own business**…which *may* include teaching others to do the same!

3. Marketing and Sales:

◊ ***Promoting Products/Services:*** Develop a marketing plan that includes online and offline strategies to promote your products or services. Use social media, email marketing, content marketing, and traditional advertising methods to reach your target audience. **Ask AI.**

◊ ***Identifying Target Audiences:*** Define your target audience based on demographics, psychographics, and behavior. Use this information to create personalized marketing campaigns that resonate with your audience. Facebook Ads have amazing tools to help you accomplish this…**perhaps they use algorithms created by AI!? You get the idea! Ask AI!**

◊ ***Closing Deals:*** Develop effective sales techniques

to close deals and convert leads into customers. This may involve building relationships, addressing objections, and offering incentives. Be confident in the skills you are building and the products and services you are delivering while **embracing technology, adapting and thriving in the process! I recommend Alex Hormozi content. Ask AI.**

4. **Problem-solving:**

◊ *Addressing Challenges:* Identify potential challenges and develop strategies to overcome them. This may involve conducting a SWOT analysis (Strengths, Weaknesses, Opportunities, Threats) to identify areas for improvement. **Ask AI.**

◊ *Finding Innovative Solutions:* Encourage creativity and innovation within yourself, first and foremost, and your team. Brainstorm ideas and explore new technologies or processes that can improve your business operations. Don't forget to **consider how partnering with AI can help you and your clients** in the process! **Ask AI.**

5. Adaptability:

◊ ***Being Open to Change:*** **Embrace change and be willing to adapt** your strategies as needed. Stay flexible and open to new ideas or approaches that can help your business grow. If you are still reading this, **this is already You!** No need to ask AI.

◊ ***Pivoting Strategies:*** If your current business model isn't working, be prepared to pivot and try new strategies. This may involve changing your target market, product offerings, or marketing tactics. Don't be afraid to try new things and iterate – that's why you are here! As *John Chaney* (RIP), former Temple Owls Men's NCAA Basketball Coach once said *"Failing is ok. Failure isn't. Better you go through the verb form than become the noun"*.

6. Networking:

◊ ***Building Relationships:*** Attend industry events, join professional organizations, and connect with other entrepreneurs to build a strong network. These connections can provide valuable support, advice, and opportunities for collaboration. Don't be afraid to ask. You can also use these opportunities to **offer your AI services** or products to them as well! See how you can collaborate, working to support each other!

◊ *Mentorship:* Seek out mentors who can offer guidance in business and/or AI specifically, who are willing to share their experiences. A mentor can provide valuable insights and help you navigate the challenges of starting a business. P.S. - Don't forget the mentees on your way to the top!

7. Resilience:

◊ *Handling Setbacks:* Expect setbacks and **be prepared to learn** from them. Use failures as opportunities to grow and improve. Remember – you can NOT grow unless you try and fail first. **If you aren't failing, you aren't trying. And as long as you keep trying…*how could you be failing?***

◊ *Persevering Through Obstacles:* Stay motivated and persistent, even when faced with challenges.

Keep your long-term goals clearly in your mind and **remain focused** on achieving them. The rest is just details. Period.

By developing these **key skills and maintaining a positive mindset**, you can embark on your entrepreneurial journey with confidence. *Trust the process and you will get there...wherever you are heading. One step at a time.*

The AI Revolution offers **countless opportunities** for innovation and growth, making it an exciting time to start your own business.

"Entrepreneurship is neither a science nor an art. It is a practice" — *Peter Drucker*

Chapter 9

AI DISCRIMINATION IS REAL

LEVELING THE PLAYING FIELD

"AI isn't going to level out equity and diversity on a playing field that they only frequent to play games" – Stefan Youngblood

Where are we Now? Where are we heading?

Know that as of 2025, we've unearthed more mud and mess in this quagmire of built-up scum of racism. Where are we today compared to December 2023? AI's footprint is larger, but its role as a **perpetuator of racial bias**, **especially against the Black community**, seems **more**

pronounced than its capacity to heal.

The case for perpetuation is **stronger**:

◊ **Biased hiring algorithms** continue to skew opportunities.

◊ **Facial recognition errors** fuel misidentification (up to 34% for darker-skinned women, per 2018 studies, with little improvement noted since), and

◊ **Economic gains** from AI **disproportionately bypass Black households** (capturing just 38 cents per dollar of new wealth, per *McKinsey*).

Healing requires **deliberate, widespread action—diverse coders, transparent systems, robust civil rights frameworks**—which **haven't scaled fast enough** in 15 months to counter the inertia of systemic bias.

Why this tilt?

AI is **NOT inherently prejudiced**—it's a mirror. The past two years have seen it reflect a society still grappling with **structural racism**, amplified by tech's homogeneity (**less than 2% Black representation** at the world's leading firms like Google) and profit-driven rollout.

Without a **radical shift** in how we build and deploy it, **AI's promise as a healer** remains **aspirational only**, while its **perpetuation of bias** remains the default. As of March 2025, what we DO know is that we're further along that default path of perpetuation than any one of transformative.

"In the solution, highlight the priority, not in the collection of the data, but the people who collect the data. That is the thing. The inclusion at the table not the books spread across the table." – Stefan Youngblood

Acknowledging the Problem

As a Lawyer handling Employment Discrimination matters for two decades now, it's not lost on me how the systemic biases that exist in our current society - disproportionately impacting various minorities, particularly members of the Black community, beyond what might appear obvious on the surface - will continue unless **acknowledged** and **addressed**. Our feelings about it are irrelevant if our actions aren't changed. This isn't a new concept.

As we navigate the AI Revolution, it's essential to recognize a significant challenge: the **inherent biases in AI training data and algorithms**. Many LLMs and AI systems are trained on data that reflect these societal biases, leading to discriminatory outcomes against these same traditionally disadvantaged minorities.

These biases manifest in various ways, from healthcare, to hiring practices to loan approvals (for individuals and businesses), **further perpetuating** existing and creating even greater, more deeply ingrained inequalities going forward.[4]

According to Dr. Deepak Chopra, shared on Jay Shetty's *On Purpose Podcast*, "AI absolutely currently has a gender and racial bias…"[5]

Potential for Worsening Discrimination

If left unaddressed, either ignored or not prioritized, the biases in AI systems could, and likely will, exacerbate existing disparities. As AI becomes more integrated into decision-making processes, which include not only the initial training data, those performing and supervising the LLMs, but also those individuals (and other AI models) regularly prompting and utilizing them in various ways, further teaching and training the LLMs the "correct"

---

[4] Stay tuned for a separate publication focused exclusively on this critical challenge faced by our **entire society**.

[5] https://www.youtube.com/watch?v=alL6EYL9bm0

questions, answers and solutions – **how could discrimination NOT increase? How could anyone be surprised?** Building upon the examples previously provided, biased AI algorithms in job recruitment could systematically overlook qualified candidates from minority backgrounds, while biased loan approval systems could deny financial opportunities to those most in need (think redlining amplified to the max). It can only be imagined the significant and negative impact that this system could have on families in these communities for generations. If you don't believe me…just **ASK AI.**

Possible Solutions

Diverse **and Representative Data Sets:** Ensuring that AI systems are trained on **diverse and representative data** sets is crucial. This can help mitigate biases and ensure that the AI systems are **fair and inclusive**. Companies and researchers must prioritize the collection and use of data that reflect the diversity of the population.

Bias Detection and Mitigation Techniques: Implementing bias detection and mitigation techniques can help identify and address biases in AI systems.

Techniques such as **fairness-aware machine learning** and **adversarial debiasing** can be employed to reduce discriminatory outcomes.

Regular audits and assessments of AI systems are not only necessary to ensure ongoing fairness, but the audits themselves **must include members of the Black community**, so that the AI systems don't continue to reflect only those people who have traditionally **excluded individuals** who don't look them.

Inclusive AI Development Teams: Creating **diverse and inclusive AI development teams** is essential for addressing biases. Teams with diverse backgrounds and perspectives are more likely to identify and address potential biases in AI systems. **Encouraging diversity** in the tech industry and **promoting inclusive hiring practices** can contribute to more equitable AI development.

The Importance of Raising Awareness

Raising awareness about the potential for AI-driven discrimination is critical. By **acknowledging the**

problem and advocating for solutions, we can work towards a more equitable future. It's essential to educate individuals, organizations, and policymakers about the risks of biased AI and the steps needed to mitigate these risks. *Silence is Violence – Anonymous*

The Role of AI in Leveling the Playing Field

While AI presents challenges, it also offers **opportunities to level the playing field** for traditionally disadvantaged minorities. AI can be leveraged to improve **access to education**, **healthcare**, and **economic opportunities**. For example, AI-driven personalized learning platforms can help bridge educational gaps, while AI-powered telehealth services can **provide access** to quality healthcare in underserved areas.

Moving Forward Addressing Bias and Discrimination

The AI Revolution holds immense potential, but it also poses significant risks if biases are not addressed. By acknowledging the problem, advocating for solutions, and leveraging AI for positive change, we can create a future where the **benefits of AI are accessible to all**. Let's work together to ensure that the AI-driven world is fair, inclusive, and equitable for everyone.

"Inclusion is not a matter of political correctness. It is the key to growth" — *Jesse Jackson*

CONCLUSION

WHAT'S THE *SMALLEST* STEP
YOU CAN TAKE NOW?

*TURNING APPREHENSION INTO
ACTION - EMBRACING THE FUTURE*

"The future belongs to those who believe in the beauty of their dreams" — *Eleanor Roosevelt*

Turning Apprehension into Action - Embracing the Future

As we conclude, let's revisit the essence of our journey through the AI Revolution. The path from fear to empowerment is paved with **knowledge, adaptability**, and an unwavering **belief** in **YOUR** ability to **grow**.

The examples provided throughout this book are only a miniscule sample among countless, yet-to-be imagined others, and a testament to the fact that *the skills you possess today hold the seeds of future opportunities*.

It's about seeing beyond the immediate (perceived) challenges, technological…but more personal— recognizing the **potential within you**, and embracing the tools and technologies that will shape the world of tomorrow.

Remember — the future is **not something to be feared** but to be shaped by our collective **will, desire,** and **curiosity**. Together, let's step into the AI era with **confidence**, optimistic and ready to transform our careers and lives, present company included.

A Future Full of Opportunities

My intention for you is to feel **empowered** and **inspired** to **embrace the opportunities** presented by the AI Revolution. You have what you need, and **you are exactly where you are supposed to be**!

Regardless of your background, education, current job

or lack thereof, there **IS a place for you** in the AI-driven world. By simply assessing your skills, talents and interests, identifying areas for growth, and embracing the benefits of lifelong learning, you can **position yourself for success** in the ever-evolving job market.

To be clear — the AI Revolution is **not just about job displacement**—it's about innovation, creativity, and limitless potential for everyone, individuals and companies included. Whether you choose to pursue traditional employment, entrepreneurship, or a combination of both, or maybe you just want to "play around" with AI, the key is to **remain adaptable** and open to **new possibilities, not just for your career, but for your life**.

Building a Collaborative Future

As we look to the future, let's continue to cultivate a mindset of **resilience**, **curiosity**, and **collaboration**. Let's leverage the power of technology to create a world where **everyone has the opportunity** to thrive and contribute their unique talents irrespective of what they look like, where they are from or current position in life!

The journey through the AI Revolution is an ongoing process. As new technologies emerge and industries evolve, continuous **learning and adaptation** will be critical. Embrace change as an **opportunity** for growth remaining **proactive** in seeking out new skills and knowledge. If you can **embrace this mindset NOW**, you can't lose.

Whether you are transitioning to a new role, starting your own business, or simply exploring the potential of AI, remember that the key to success lies in your **mindset** and **willingness** to learn. By staying **curious, open-minded**, and **resilient**, you can navigate the challenges of the AI era and **seize the opportunities** that come your way.

IF you are still reading this, I have Faith in You!

Final Thoughts

Thank you for embarking on this journey with me. Together, let's shape a future where the **possibilities** are **endless**, with the only limit being our individual and collective **imaginations**. I'm here for it...unless or until I'm replaced!

"Courage is being afraid...and doing it ANYWAY"

APPENDIX

PERSONAL
AI JOB SHIFT
SKILLS WORKSHEET

See How YOU ALREADY Fit In!

INSTRUCTIONS

Use this worksheet to:

(i) **IDENTIFY** your current job and skills (even if <u>not</u> utilized in current job),

(ii) **ENVISION** *potential* AI future roles, *<u>AND</u>*

(iii) **CREATE** YOUR Opportunity!

Follow prompts below to complete each section.

SEE EXAMPLE AT BOTTOM FOR GUIDANCE

A. Current Job Position/Title: _____

B. Current Skills: (List below **<u>TOP 5</u>** skills even if not utilized in current Job - **<u>NO</u>** Skill is TOO Small to List! Use no more than three (3) words to describe each skill):[6]

    1. _____

    2. _____

    3. _____

    4. _____

    5. _____

---

[6] Skill Examples: diligent, focused, adaptable, empathetic, compassionate, team-oriented, builder, leader, resilient, tenacious, etc.

C. Potential/Desired AI-Job Positions/Titles:

    1. _____

    2. _____

    3. _____

    4. _____

    5. _____

D. Potential AI-Job Required Skills:

    1. _____

    2. _____

    3. _____

    4. _____

    5. _____

E. Bridging the Gap: Combine + List below AND Consider *Any and ALL* *Potentially* Transferable Skills from Sections "*B*" and "*D*" Above:

    ⇒ "(B)" Current Skills:

    1. _____

    2. _____

    3. _____

    ⇒ "(D)" Potential AI-Job Required Skills:

    1. _____

    2. _____

    3. _____

F. Skill Acquisition: Identify the <u>Top Five (5)</u> *New* <u>Skills</u> necessary to acquire any of the Potential AI-Job Positions/Titles identified in Section "C" Above

1. _____
2. _____
3. _____
4. _____
5. _____

G. Action Plan:

I. <u>Skill Development</u>: Describe *ONLY Three (3)* Specific Actions YOU will take to develop any required *NEW* skills, etc.:

1. _____
2. _____
3. _____

II. <u>Minimum Resources Needed</u>: List *ONLY Three (3)* Resources (*e.g.*, free/paid courses, YouTube Channels, Industry-Specific Leaders, Certifications, books, mentors by name) you <u>will</u> utilize:

1. _____
2. _____
3. _____

III. Timeline: Set a timeline for <u>Your</u> Action Plan (to Acquire any New Skills and Opportunities):

⇒ Start Date: _____

⇒ Milestones: _____

⇒ Target Completion Date: _____

H. Reflection:

◊ What are your **motivations** for transitioning to this new role?

_____

_____

_____

_____

◊ How do you **envision** this new role impacting your career and personal life?

_____

_____

_____

_____

◊ What challenges do you anticipate, and how will you address them?

_____

_____

_____

_____

Pro Tip: By anticipating potential challenges in advance, you are priming your brain to subconsciously begin overcoming them, better positioning you to "hit the ground running" if/when they present themselves.

(SEE EXAMPLE ON FOLLOWING PAGES)

EXAMPLE

A. Current Job Position/Title: Retail Sales Associate

B. Current Skills:
1. Customer service
2. Product knowledge
3. Sales techniques
4. Cash handling
5. Inventory management

C. Potential/Desired AI-Job Positions/Titles: AI Retail Analyst

D. Potential AI-Job Required Skills:
1. Data analysis
2. AI tools for inventory management
3. Customer data analytics
4. Trend forecasting
5. Digital marketing strategies

E. Bridging the Gap: Combine + List Below AND Consider _Any and ALL_ _Potentially_ Transferable Skills from Sections "*B*" and "*D*" Above:
6. (B) Current Skills:
    1. Customer service
    2. Product knowledge
    3. Sales techniques

7. (D) Potential AI-Job Required Skills:
    4. Data analysis
    5. AI tools for inventory management
    6. Trend forecasting

F. Skill Acquisition: Identify the Top Five (5) <u>New Skills</u> necessary to acquire any of the Potential AI-Job Positions/Titles identified in Section "C" Above

1. Advanced data analysis techniques
2. AI inventory management systems
3. Predictive customer analytics
4. Trend forecasting methods
5. Digital marketing automation tools

G. Action Plan:
I. Skill Development:
⇒ Enroll in a data analysis course

⇒ Learn to use AI inventory management tools

⇒ Study trend forecasting methods

II. Resources Needed:
⇒ Online courses on data analysis

⇒ Tutorials on AI tools

⇒ Books on trend forecasting

III. Timeline:

⇒ Start Date: August 1, 2025

⇒ Milestones: Complete data analysis course by October 2025, gain proficiency in AI tools by December 2025

⇒ Target Completion Date: January 31, 2025

H. Reflection:

◊ **Motivations**: Desire to stay relevant in the evolving job market, interest in AI technologies, empowering self

◊ **Impact**: Enhance career prospects, increase job satisfaction, empower community

◊ **Challenges**: Time management while learning new skills, adapting to new technologies

NOTES PAGE

NOTES PAGE

ABOUT THE AUTHOR

Jared A. Jacobson, Esq. is a lawyer by trade practicing primarily in the areas of Labor & Employment, Business Transactions and Commercial Real Estate with two decades of experience and a strong interest in and passion for Artificial Intelligence, Web3, Blockchain and Emerging Technology. Jared has been operating *Jared Jacobson Law, LLC* since September 2009.

Having navigated the complexities of the job market and the transformative impacts of the AI Revolution, Jared is dedicated to empowering individuals to adapt and thrive in an AI-driven world.

Jared's insights and strategies are aimed at helping people recognize and seize the opportunities presented by technological advancements regardless of education, demographic and starting point in life, without the fear many have around "AI"…or just learning new skills and having fun.

Jared is admitted to practice law in New York, New Jersey and Pennsylvania, as well as several federal courts, and the United States Supreme Court.

Jared has three amazing, beautiful children and dedicates this book to them…as well as all of the other children out there who may not have otherwise had the same opportunities but now just may, with the AI Revolution among us. With Peace and Gratitude…what a time to be alive!

STAY CONNECTED + TAKE ACTION

⇒ **Leave a Quick Review**
Scan or visit: AIJobShift.com/book-review

⇒ **Join the AI Job Shift Newsletter**
Stay in the loop with exclusive updates, live training sessions, and future products and services.
Scan or visit: AIJobShift.com/newsletter

⇒ **Earn While You Share**
Resonate with this mission? Join our affiliate program and help spread the word.
Scan or visit: AIJobShift.com/affiliate-program

JARED A. JACOBSON, ESQ.